marijuana today

# Marijuana's Harmful Effects on Youth

# marijuana today

# Marijuana's Harmful Effects on Youth

Julie Nelson

MASON CREST

Mason Crest
450 Parkway Drive, Suite D
Broomall, Pennsylvania 19008
(866) MCP-BOOK (toll-free)
www.masoncrest.com

First printing
9 8 7 6 5 4 3 2 1

ISBN (hardback) 978-1-4222-4107-3
ISBN (series) 978-1-4222-4103-5
ISBN (ebook) 978-1-4222-7695-2

Cataloging-in-Publication Data on file with the Library of Congress

**NATIONAL HIGHLIGHTS**

Developed and Produced by National Highlights Inc.
Editor: Andrew Morkes
Interior and cover design: Yolanda Van Cooten
Proofreader: Mika Jin
Production: Michelle Luke

# contents

**KEY ICONS TO LOOK FOR:**

**Words to understand:** These words with their easy-to-understand definitions will increase the reader's understanding of the text while building vocabulary skills.

**Sidebars:** This boxed material within the main text allows readers to build knowledge, gain insights, explore possibilities, and broaden their perspectives by weaving together additional information to provide realistic and holistic perspectives.

**Educational Videos:** Readers can view videos by scanning our QR codes, providing them with additional educational content to supplement the text. Examples include news coverage, moments in history, speeches, iconic sports moments and much more!

**Text-dependent questions:** These questions send the reader back to the text for more careful attention to the evidence presented there.

**Research projects:** Readers are pointed toward areas of further inquiry connected to each chapter. Suggestions are provided for projects that encourage deeper research and analysis.

**Series glossary of key terms:** This back-of-the-book glossary contains terminology used throughout this series. Words found here increase the reader's ability to read and comprehend higher-level books and articles in this field.

# Introduction

In the past decade, public opinion regarding marijuana legalization has begun to change around the world. A growing number of countries have legalized the medical use of cannabis to treat pain and nausea, as well as seizure disorders, Crohn's disease, and other diseases and medical conditions. Countries that have legalized medical cannabis in recent years include the United States (in a majority of states), Canada, Australia, Spain, Portugal, Jamaica, Colombia, the Czech Republic, Switzerland, Romania, Germany, India, Israel, Macedonia, South Africa, and Uruguay.

A small, but growing, number of countries have also legalized or decriminalized the use of recreational cannabis by adults. Recreational use of cannabis has been decriminalized in the United Kingdom, Ireland, France, Denmark, Italy, Spain, Czech Republic, Germany, and other countries, although it is still technically illegal. In the United States, eight states have legalized recreational cannabis for adult use: Alaska, California, Colorado, Maine, Massachusetts, Nevada, Oregon, and Washington.

Although the use of marijuana by adults has been legalized or decriminalized in many countries, it's important to note that the use of marijuana—just like alcohol, cigarettes, or even fatty foods— can cause various side effects and health issues. In this book, we will look at how marijuana affects the growing body and mind, with an emphasis on teenagers. You will learn why doctors strongly advise anyone under the age of twenty-one (some doctors advise age twenty-five) to avoid using marijuana. Armed with new knowledge about the harmful effects of marijuana—as well as evidence of its benefits for some medical conditions—you will be able to make an educated decision about whether or not you should try marijuana once you are an adult.

Marijuana has serious effects on the human brain, and it's important for teens to know what the side effects are and how they will affect them as adults. In chapter one, you will learn about the negative mental effects of marijuana—from memory problems and attention problems, to lower school and job achievement, to even addiction. You will also learn about the symptoms of cannabis intoxication and withdrawal, as well as cannabis use disorder.

Chapter two discusses marijuana's negative physical effects on the human body—ranging from elevated blood pressure and heart rate, loss of control over motor functions, damage to the lungs and brain, and even overdose.

Chapter three covers a variety of topics ranging from the differences between recreational marijuana and medical marijuana; how marijuana products (marijuana flower, oils, tinctures, edibles, etc.) affect each person differently; marijuana dependence and addiction; withdrawal symptoms that may occur if a person quits using marijuana; and what to do if you think someone you love or care about is addicted to marijuana.

In chapter four, we will talk about how marijuana laws and public opinion about the use of marijuana are changing in the United States and around the world, how parents make decisions to treat their sick children with medical marijuana, and the personal choice adults make about using medical and/or recreational marijuana.

In chapter five, we'll talk about the science of marijuana, including how people study marijuana and its effects; medical migrants and cannabidiol; how the federal U.S. government views medical marijuana science; and how medical marijuana has helped some people with diseases and disorders such as epilepsy and post-traumatic stress disorder, as well as Holocaust survivors.

While many people consider medical marijuana to be a "wonder drug," it's important to understand both the positive and negative effects of marijuana, which can be especially harmful to youth. So, let's gets the facts and begin learning.

*There is no doubt that using marijuana can negatively affect a person's mental and emotional state.*

## words to understand

**delusion:** A strong erroneous belief that is not based on fact or reality. Someone who is having delusions may be convinced that a person wants to hurt them when they do not.

**marijuana dispensary:** A store where people can buy medical marijuana legally in some countries or in certain U.S. states.

**mental side effects:** Feelings and beliefs of people that are caused by or changed by marijuana use.

**psychotic episode:** A serious mental event that involves a loss of connection to reality. Those who are having psychotic episodes may hallucinate (seeing something that is not there) and/or have delusions.

**secondhand smoke:** Smoke breathed out by users and then breathed in by nearby adults or children who are not smoking.

# chapter 1

# The Effects of Marijuana on the Mental Health of Teens

There is no doubt that using marijuana can negatively affect a person's mental and emotional state. Despite its growing popularity and legalization in some states in the United States and other countries, marijuana can also be addictive. The risk of mental addiction is one of the most important things to consider, even when using marijuana as an adult. Because the teen brain is still growing, it is unsafe for teens to use marijuana or be exposed to **secondhand smoke** from marijuana at any time. All states and other countries have passed marijuana laws designed to keep young people away from marijuana.

*Colorado was the first state in the U.S. to legalize marijuana for recreational use, but it is illegal for people under age twenty-one to buy, have, or use it.*

What are the harmful mental effects of marijuana use, and what can teens learn about marijuana that can help them avoid marijuana use? This chapter answers these questions and focuses on the mental health effects of marijuana on teens.

## Did You Know?

- In 2016, about 24 percent of tenth graders reported that they had used marijuana in the past year. About 9.5 percent of eighth graders reported doing so.
- Ten percent of people who use marijuana may become addicted to it.
- Of those who start using marijuana in their teens, 17 percent are likely to become addicted.

Source: National Institute on Drug Abuse

## The Mental Effects of Marijuana

There are many **mental side effects** of marijuana use that may harm the growing human brain and cause teens to act in unusual ways. One of the problems with making marijuana legal for everyone is that each person is affected differently by marijuana. One person may feel fine after using marijuana, while another person who uses the same amount may feel anxiety or have other mental health issues. Because marijuana use affects people differently, it is important to keep it out of the hands of young adults and teenagers, or provide a safe environment for medical marijuana treatments if it is recommended by a doctor.

Marijuana use affects some areas of the brain more strongly than others, and its use may cause hallucinations (seeing things that aren't there), **delusions**, or risky behavior in some people and young adults. The areas of the brain that are most affected by cannabis are the cerebellum (the part of the brain that controls balance and the coordination of muscles and the body), the basal ganglia (which processes information on movement and performs other functions), and the cerebral cortex (the area of the brain that is responsible for thought, perception, and the producing and understanding of language). The reason these areas of the brain respond to marijuana is that they have the most cannabinoid receptors. These little receptors are located throughout the body and the brain, but most of them are in the cerebellum, the basal ganglia, and the cerebral cortex.

Common mental side effects of marijuana include:

- Memory problems
- Attention problems
- Lower school or job achievement
- Bad judgement in social situations or while driving
- Addiction

These are not good side effects, and since the potency (strength) of marijuana can be hard to measure, there is no guarantee that a marijuana product will affect everyone the same way. For this and legal reasons, teens should not use marijuana until they are adults. (Adults who use marijuana should be sure to check the potency of any product that they purchase.) Another reason not to use marijuana: legal fines and punishments for marijuana use can have lasting effects on your life, just like using any illegal drug.

*Lower academic achievement is a common mental side effect of marijuana usage.*

# Marijuana Opinions and Usage

The National Institute on Drug Abuse, which is part of the U.S. National Institutes of Health, reports that more than eleven million young adults (ages eighteen to twenty-five) in the United States use marijuana at least once a year. It also found that negative opinions about marijuana use are lessening as marijuana is legalized in more states and countries. However, this does not mean that more teens and children are using marijuana. In fact, many studies in marijuana-legal states such as Colorado and California indicate that fewer teens are using marijuana since it was legalized, or at least use has not increased. The increasing availability of marijuana in cities across the world means that it is around teens and young adults more, although laws keep them from buying it legally.

*Learn more about the negative effects of marijuana on the teenage brain, and the debate about legalization:*

## What Happens to Your Brain When You Use Marijuana?

When marijuana is smoked or vaporized, the THC passes from your lungs into your bloodstream, which carries it to your brain and other organs. (THC is a chemical found in marijuana that alters people's mental state.) THC attaches to cannabinoid receptors, which are a part of the endocannabinoid system. This system regulates the brain's development and function and helps control appetite, pain, mood, and memory. The effects of marijuana will take a bit longer (about an hour) to kick in if you eat or drink marijuana, but it will have the same effects on the user in time. The effects of marijuana on your brain and body may last one to three hours, and even longer if you consumed the marijuana by eating or drinking.

Marijuana usually causes feelings of pleasure called a "high" as it releases dopamine into the brain's reward centers. Dopamine is a naturally occurring chemical in the human body that increases pleasurable feelings in the mind and body. This is the feeling people seek when they smoke or consume recreational marijuana, although medical users may seek to create these same feelings for the relief of pain.

## Mental Health Issues Associated with Marijuana Use

Since marijuana affects each person differently, it's often difficult to predict how it will affect one person as compared to another. Nevertheless, reports of teens being rushed to hospitals or calling 911 for help after consuming marijuana do happen. A more serious reaction often occurs when marijuana with higher THC content is used.

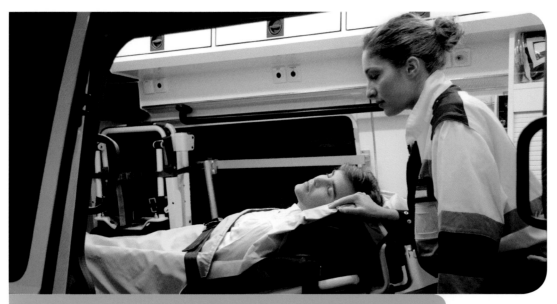

*Overconsumption of cannabis can cause serious side effects, which may result in a trip to the emergency room.*

15

# Colorado's Teen Marijuana Laws

Colorado was the first state in the U.S. to legalize marijuana for recreational use. This means that an adult does not need a prescription from a doctor or other health care professional to buy and use marijuana in a private residence or at a private event. In Colorado, anyone who has valid identification can go into a **marijuana dispensary** and buy one ounce (28.3495 grams) of marijuana each day. By law, shops may not be located too close to schools, and all schools have rules in place to punish or expel teens who bring marijuana to school. If a student is over the age of eighteen, then he or she can face a civil penalty (fine). Depending on how much marijuana or marijuana concentrate (oil, wax, budder, shatter) a teen has, and whether the marijuana was given to another teen or adult, the fines may be $100 or more, and the individual may also have to serve jail time.

At times, teen and adult marijuana users may hallucinate. This is the result of marijuana's effects on the human brain. Marijuana concentrates may cause **psychotic episodes** because they are more potent (stronger) than other forms of marijuana. For instance, smoking or vaping marijuana extracts make them stronger by giving the user more THC at once. (Vaping involves inhaling the active ingredients of marijuana via vapors created by heating, but not burning, cannabis.)

## Cannabis Intoxication, Withdrawal, and Cannabis Use Disorder

Cannabis intoxication follows the use of marijuana. A person who is intoxicated by cannabis may have a "high" feeling, trouble with physical movement or feel less coordinated, experience anxiety, believe that time is moving slowly, demonstrate bad judgment and risky behavior, and withdraw from social situations. Intoxication may also cause red eyes, a strong desire to eat or drink, dry mouth, and a faster heartbeat (tachycardia). Hallucinations may occur.

*People who have been diagnosed with cannabis use disorder may have trouble in school.*

*The abuse of cannabis can cause insomnia and other negative side effects.*

Withdrawal from using marijuana can increase feelings of irritability, anger, or anxiety, or cause loss of sleep, less desire to eat, depression, restlessness, pain in or around the stomach, shakiness, sweating, fever, chills, or a headache. Withdrawal symptoms can last about a week.

Cannabis use disorder (CUD) is a condition that was discovered in 2016, and that the National Institutes of Health (NIH) states is "common and often untreated." NIH notes that CUD can be part of other addictive disorders, as well as problems with behavior and disabilities. CUD is a mental health problem with eleven symptoms:

1. Consuming more marijuana than you meant to
2. Wanting to consume less marijuana or stop using it, but being unable to
3. Spending a lot of time getting, using, or recovering from marijuana
4. Getting cravings or urges to use marijuana
5. Being unable to do schoolwork or work because of marijuana use
6. Continuing to use marijuana even when it causes relationship problems
7. Giving up important social, work, or recreational activities to use marijuana
8. Using marijuana repeatedly, even if it puts you in danger
9. Continuing to use marijuana even when a physical or mental problem is worse when you use
10. Needing more marijuana to get the effect you want
11. Withdrawal symptoms

Having two or three of these symptoms means that you have mild CUD. Four or five means you have a moderate disorder, and six or more mean the CUD is severe. A medical study found that many adults with CUD do not get treatment for this disorder. Because teens are not legally allowed to use marijuana, it is unknown how many teens have the disorder.

## Other Disorders

There are several other disorders that are caused by using marijuana: cannabis intoxication delirium, cannabis-induced psychotic disorder, cannabis-induced anxiety disorder, cannabis-induced sleep disorder, and unspecified cannabis-related disorder. These disorders can be diagnosed in teens and adults who use marijuana, and each have their own symptoms and side effects.

# Laws That Prevent Teens from Using Marijuana

Every U.S. state that sells legal medical or recreational marijuana has laws against selling or giving marijuana to teens. These laws also prevent adults from using marijuana around children. The purpose of these laws is to keep teens from using marijuana when they are not old enough to handle the side effects, or when the side effects could cause problems in their lives with relationships, addiction, anxiety, learning, concentration, or work or schoolwork. Like the choice to use alcohol, the choice to use marijuana is best made by an adult over the age of eighteen, or, in most states and some countries, twenty-one. While the side effects of marijuana are often less damaging to teens than the side effects of alcohol, there are still very real dangers that can affect teens using marijuana, including driving while intoxicated (which can cause injury or death to themselves and others), and heightened feelings of anxiety, depression, or fear caused by other mental health disorders. The American Academy of Pediatrics, a group of pediatricians that focuses on child and teen health, reports that the human brain keeps developing through the early twenties, and that teens who use marijuana ten times or more a month may cause permanent or temporary changes to their memories or planning functions. They may also lose intelligence quotient (I.Q.) points and increase their chances of addiction later in life. Medical marijuana may be prescribed to teens when approved by parents and a doctor, or two doctors in some states. Otherwise, it is illegal for adults under the age of twenty-one (eighteen in some states) to use marijuana.

*Every U.S. state that sells legal medical or recreational marijuana has laws against selling or giving marijuana to teens.*

## text-dependent questions

1. What are common side effects for teens who use marijuana?
2. Why is it dangerous for teens to use marijuana?
3. What age do you have to be to use marijuana in the United States?

## research project

Learn more about cannabis use disorder, cannabis intoxication delirium, cannabis-induced psychotic disorder, cannabis-induced anxiety disorder, and other disorders. Write a one-paragraph summary that describes each disorder and its symptoms.

*Lung and breathing problems are just a few of the negative physical side effects of using marijuana.*

## words to understand

**addiction:** A disease of the brain in which a person has an overwhelming desire to use drugs, alcohol, or other substances, or engage in harmful acts or behaviors.

**bronchodilation:** The expansion of the bronchial air passages in the respiratory tract.

**chronic obstructive pulmonary disease:** An umbrella term used to describe several types of progressive lung diseases.

**concentration:** Focusing your attention on one thing.

**decriminalize:** To reduce or get rid of punishments for the possession and use of small amounts of cannabis.

**physical effects:** The effects of a substance or action on the body.

# chapter 2

# The Effects of Marijuana on the Physical Health of Teens

Cannabis has been legalized or **decriminalized** for use by adults in some U.S. states and more than twenty other countries. Medical marijuana use involves using marijuana, concentrates, or extracts to treat pain or symptoms from chemotherapy, epilepsy, Crohn's disease, post-traumatic stress syndrome, and other diseases, disorders, or treatments. Many people use recreational marijuana to relax and otherwise feel good. While there are many good aspects of marijuana that is used responsibly by adults, or recommended by physicians for medical use for adults and children, it is important to remember that marijuana has harmful physical side effects, which we'll discuss in this chapter.

## The Physical Effects of Marijuana Use on Teens

Although many think of the "high" feeling people get when they use marijuana, there are many **physical effects** on the body, as well. These effects are just as important to health as the mental effects. The physical effects on the body, which apply to anyone who uses or accidentally consumes marijuana, include:

- Red eyes
- Dry mouth
- Higher heart rate
- Lung and breathing problems
- Problems with **concentration**
- Reduced motor control and balance
- Unwanted weight loss
- May make puberty come later in young men or affect sperm production

*After recreational marijuana was legalized in Colorado, public officials worried that the number of teens using marijuana would increase. In fact, studies show that marijuana use among Colorado teens is becoming less popular since legalization.*

# Decreasing Teen Marijuana Use

Although marijuana use has increased among adults (or at least more adults are reporting that they use marijuana following legalization and reduced criminal penalties for marijuana use), teenagers in Colorado have reported the same or less marijuana use than before it was legalized. In the 2015 Healthy Kids Colorado Survey (a health survey that gathers information about Colorado's kids and young adults), 62 percent of middle school and high school students reported that they had never used marijuana, but 30 percent said they had used alcohol within the past month. In 2009, the rate of teen marijuana use was 24.8 percent. In 2015 it was 19.7 percent, showing that marijuana use is becoming less popular among teens after legalization. Additionally, tobacco (cigarettes and chewing tobacco) use continues to decline as more and more teens become aware of the harmful effects of tobacco on the body.

- May potentially affect young women's menstrual cycles
- More risk for problems in unborn babies

Let's discuss a few of these physical effects in more detail in the following paragraphs:

## Higher Heart Rate

A higher heart rate makes the body work harder to keep up, and after inhaling marijuana smoke, the lung passages (which take in air) and blood vessels expand. An increased heart rate can affect people differently, and mixing marijuana and other drugs, even drugs prescribed by doctors for illnesses or anxiety, can make people act strangely or feel unwell. According to the American Heart Association, symptoms and conditions caused by a fast heart rate (known as tachycardia) include:

- Fainting
- Lightheadedness or dizziness
- A fluttering feeling in the chest
- Chest pain
- Pressure or tightness
- Shortness of breath
- Fatigue/tiredness
- Unconsciousness (in extreme cases)
- Cardiac arrest (in extreme cases)

## Damage to the Lungs

Marijuana smoke is harmful to the lungs, and it can cause a harsh cough that does not go away for many marijuana users. Smoking a lot of marijuana may cause lung problems such as:

- Asthma
- **Chronic Obstructive Pulmonary Disease**
- Bronchitis
- Pneumonia

The association between smoking marijuana and lung cancer remains unclear. Some well-designed and large-scale studies have failed to identify any increased risk of lung cancer in people who have smoked marijuana. But the Alcohol & Drug Abuse Institute at the University of Washington reports that "no study has definitively ruled out the possibility that some individuals, especially heavier marijuana users, may incur an elevated risk of cancer. This risk appears to be smaller than for tobacco, yet is important to consider when weighing the benefits and risks of smoking marijuana." Medical marijuana may also help some lung conditions (by reducing airway inflammation and causing **bronchodilation**), so results may vary.

*Smoking large amounts of marijuana can cause lung problems such as asthma, bronchitis, pneumonia, and Chronic Obstructive Pulmonary Disease.*

# Helping Teens Make Safe Decisions About Marijuana

The National Institute on Drug Abuse, a U.S. federal government research institute, recommends that parents talk with their children and teens about drug use to prevent **addiction**. Here are some things parents might ask their kids about marijuana:

1. What have you heard about marijuana?
2. What are some effects of using marijuana?
3. How do you feel about marijuana use?
4. Have you been offered marijuana? If so, what did you say?

Teens should feel comfortable asking their parents (or another adult, such as a school counselor or a therapist) about marijuana. Signs that other teens may be using marijuana include:

- Dizziness
- Red eyes or using eye drops often
- Being angry or irritated more often
- Lack of interest in usual activities
- Memory problems

It's important to remember that regular marijuana use can lead to addiction for some people, and certainly dependence, just like alcohol abuse. Marijuana addiction is not as severe as other types of addiction, but many people experience side effects when they stop heavy use of marijuana. Marijuana can cause people to lose interest in activities they enjoyed before in favor of using. Marijuana may also affect teens mentally by reducing learning ability, memory, and the ability to concentrate, or by causing negative emotional changes.

## Damage to the Brain

Researchers believe the human brain keeps growing and changing until we are age twenty-five or even older, so using marijuana as a teenager can negatively affect your brain. Marijuana has negative effects on memory, learning, and intelligence, and these effects can be long-term and even permanent in those who began using marijuana regularly as teens. The National Institute on Drug Abuse reports that some scientific studies have found significant structural differences between the brains of people who do and do not use the drug, while others have not. More research must be conducted to establish the negative effects of marijuana on the brain.

## Physical Marijuana Withdrawal Symptoms

Physical withdrawal symptoms from quitting heavy marijuana use are not as intense as those experienced when quitting heavy drinking, heroin use, or the use of other, more addictive drugs like methamphetamine. But there will still be serious physical withdrawal symptoms, including:

- Insomnia
- Restlessness
- Irritability and unprovoked anger
- Anxiety
- Low appetite or rapid weight loss
- Stomach pain
- Cold sweats
- Shakiness
- Fever
- Chills
- Headaches

Withdrawal symptoms can last about a week. Medical studies have shown that withdrawal symptoms become more intense if the user has used the drug for a long time. Teens suffering from marijuana withdrawal are more likely than adults to experience problems at school or work, in relationships, or with managing money. They also often experience depression.

*If a friend or family member is angry and irritated more often, frequently has red eyes, is uninterested in hobbies or life in general, and has memory problems, he or she may be abusing marijuana.*

## Marijuana Overdose

Some people who use too much marijuana have overdosed. An overdosing person may experience:

- Panic attacks
- Uncontrolled shaking
- Rapid heartbeat
- High blood pressure
- Unresponsiveness (passed out or zombie-like)
- Hallucinations
- Mental confusion

Marijuana overdose is different from overdose from cocaine or opioids. The area of the brain that responds to marijuana doesn't control life functions such as breathing. As far as science knows currently, people don't die from marijuana overdose directly. But that doesn't mean that it's not dangerous in high doses. You can still overdose—and there are very negative results.

ProjectKnow.com, an addiction information website, reports that "if the marijuana is laced with other drugs, some common adverse effects can include seizures, strokes, or irregular heartbeats."

*Watch the effects of marijuana on drivers:*

# Driving Under the Influence of Marijuana

Driving after or while using marijuana is very unsafe. It is dangerous to the driver and his or her passengers, dangerous for other people on the road, and dangerous to pedestrians. Driving under the influence of marijuana is illegal and against the law in every state in the United States, as well as in many countries. Driving after using marijuana has been shown to reduce judgement, cause less control over the body, and lessen reaction time to dangerous situations that may happen while you are driving. Marijuana is the drug found most often in drivers who have caused or been in car crashes, including crashes where people have died. In Europe, drivers with THC in their blood were twice as likely to be responsible for car crashes than drivers who had not used marijuana or alcohol before driving. Drivers who use both marijuana and alcohol before driving are even more likely to cause a car crash.

Because marijuana legalization has increased the number of states and countries where it is legal to use marijuana, more adults are using marijuana and driving. It is always illegal to drive while under the influence of marijuana, and police departments are working on a breathalyzer that can tell whether a person has used marijuana.

As a teen, you should never use marijuana (unless it is recommended by a doctor for a medical condition). But, if for some reason you decide to use marijuana, you should never drive after using it. Find another way to get to your destination. This way, you stay safe, your passengers are not in danger, and no one else on the road is in danger, either. And you won't go to jail if you get caught driving under the influence.

*Driving after using marijuana is extremely dangerous. Cannabis use reduces judgement, causes less control over the body, and lessens reaction time.*

## text-dependent questions

1. What are some of the physical effects of marijuana on the human body?
2. Does the use of marijuana cause lung cancer?
3. What happens during a marijuana overdose?

## research project

Research how marijuana affects teens. How much information can you find? Do you think teens should use marijuana? Why or why not?

*Cannabis has been used in what is now India since 2000 B.C.E.*

## words to understand

**gateway drug:** A drug or substance that leads to the use of more dangerous drugs.

**mental dependence:** Mental reactions to the use of a drug or substance, or withdrawal from it.

**physical dependence:** Physical reactions to the use of a drug or substance, or withdrawal from it.

**symptoms:** A physical or mental feeling that may be the result of a condition such as addiction or a disease.

**withdrawal:** Stopping the use of a drug or other substance that may be addictive.

# chapter 3

# Marijuana Use, Dependence, and Quitting

## Teens and Marijuana Use

Teen use of marijuana is illegal in the United States and other countries, but this does not mean that teens do not use it. It is hard to measure the number of teens who use marijuana because it is illegal. This means that teens may not tell the truth about marijuana use, or may use it when they are away from their parents, teachers, or other adults. But a study of teens aged twelve to seventeen by the Substance Abuse and Mental Health Services Administration found that fewer and fewer teens believe that smoking marijuana causes great risk. The percentage of teens with this belief has increased since 2010. As doctors and pediatricians (child and teen doctors) point out, marijuana can be harmful to the growing brain, and should be avoided until the legal marijuana use age of eighteen or twenty-one (depending on where one lives).

## Recreational Marijuana Use vs. Medical Marijuana Use

There are two different reasons for using marijuana. We most often associate marijuana with recreational use (hanging out with friends, attending social events, parties, or concerts, relaxing at home after a hard day's work, etc.), but marijuana is increasingly being used to treat a variety of ailments and **symptoms**. In this section, we'll discuss the difference between recreational marijuana use and medical marijuana use.

### Recreational Marijuana Use

Recreational marijuana is used for relaxation and enjoyment. Some people believe that using marijuana makes activities like concerts, movies, athletic events, or just hanging out with friends more fun. For some, marijuana can cause less social anxiety (the fear of interaction with others), and for some it may cause other issues. Whatever the effects of marijuana are for you, only use it when you are of legal age, in a state or country where it is legal to do so, and in a safe situation (i.e., you are not planning to drive, etc.). Recreational marijuana use is for adults only, although many people experiment with marijuana while they are teenagers. There are physical and mental dangers and problems that are associated with recreational and medical marijuana use. The developing brain should be protected from those effects because we don't yet know what they all are. Future medical studies are the only way to find out how marijuana use at a young age can affect the brain.

*Edibles, such as this marijuana cake, have become popular methods of consuming cannabis.*

# Teen Marijuana Use in Colorado

In Colorado, the first state to legalize recreational (or adult-use) marijuana, one out of every five teens say they use marijuana at least once a month. This number was the same before adult-use marijuana was legalized in the state. Most teens in Colorado do not use marijuana, and never have, but most teens use alcohol. Tobacco use for teens has gone down, and many teens also use prescription drugs without a prescription, which could lead to dangerous opioid or other types of abuse. Some teens get marijuana from a person who has a medical marijuana card (a document issued by a government that indicates that a patient may use, buy, or have medical cannabis at home, on his or her person, or both) or they buy it on the black market.

## Medical Marijuana Use

Medical marijuana use is a different situation. In many places in the world, medical marijuana has been used legally or illegally for centuries to treat different diseases, chronic pain, and the side effects of medical treatments, as well as for enjoyment. In most U.S. states, medical marijuana can only be bought with a prescription or "recommendation" from a doctor or other health care professional. Medical marijuana has been legalized or decriminalized (to reduce or get rid of punishments for an act, such as possessing marijuana, that is against the law) in more than half of U.S. states and more than twenty countries because medical studies have found that it can help reduce disease symptoms. It can also be used to treat side effects of other medical treatments, such as feelings of nausea (being sick to your stomach) or loss of appetite caused by cancer radiation treatments. Medical marijuana in the form of cannabidiol (CBD) oil has also been shown to help those with severe seizure disorders such as Dravet Syndrome. CBD is a chemical compound found in the cannabis plant that is non-psychoactive. A study published in the *New England*

# Medical Marijuana in India

The sacred Hindu texts known as The Vedas feature one of the first mentions of cannabis in recorded history. They were written as far back as 2000 B.C.E. Cannabis was one of five sacred plants and known as "the joy-giver and liberator." The Hindu people used cannabis to help experience delight and lose fear, or inhibition, releasing them from anxiety and worry. Marijuana is called "bhang" in India, and Hindus believe that the god Shiva found the marijuana plant after falling asleep under it after an argument with his family. Shiva both ate and drank marijuana and was known as the Lord of Bhang. Cannabis is still used in drinks in India today. It is boiled and combined with almonds, pistachios, poppy seeds, pepper, ginger, sugar, and milk or yogurt. Bhang can also be rolled up into small balls and eaten. Ganja is also eaten in India. It is made from the flowers and upper leaves of the marijuana plant. Charas, which is made from blooming flowers, is essentially hashish and contains resin. It is smoked in a pipe called a chillum, and shared among two to five people.

*Journal of Medicine* showed that CBD oil can cut the number of seizures in a child with Dravet Syndrome in half. Five percent of those studied stopped having seizures completely. The placebo group in this study had no significant reduction.

## The Different Effects of Marijuana Products

Just as in India, there are many different marijuana products on the market today. Options include marijuana flower, oils, tinctures, wax, shatter, and food and drinks prepared with cannabis (or cannabis butter in some cases). Marijuana products have different effects on different people, but some products are also designed to be much stronger than others, and are more likely to be hard to handle for any teen or adult. For this reason, even medical marijuana should be used with caution and

*Shatter is a form of cannabis concentrate that looks like colored glass. It typically has much higher THC content (the component of cannabis that makes people feel "high") than other types of marijuana products.*

# The Potential Dangers of Marijuana Concentrates

Although marijuana flower may have about the same potency (the amount of THC that alters a user's mental state) as it did half a century ago, the levels of THC are much higher in marijuana concentrates. Through scientific extraction methods, the THC and CBD are removed from the marijuana plant leaves and flower and made into liquids or solids that are then consumed by smoking, vaping, or as oils and tinctures added to drinks and foods.

Think of concentrates as extracts of the cannabis plant, just like vanilla or anise extracts used in cooking. There are many names for marijuana concentrates, such as shatter, rosin, BHO, CO2, crumble, honey oil, wax, dabs, hash, hashish, tinctures, honeycomb, and sap. These marijuana concentrates are created by using a scientific extraction method, frequently using carbon dioxide, alcohol, butane, hydrocarbons, or propane. These components are called solvents. Marijuana can also be extracted using solventless methods, which use water or heat. These methods are considered safer as it is unknown how solvents might affect the marijuana extract consumer. It is important to note that, while cannabis flowers usually have 10 to 25 percent THC, cannabis concentrates usually have between 50 to 80 percent THC. The THC content may even be as high as 90 percent. This makes concentrates much stronger and harder to dose by doctors and patients. Concentrates may also be more addictive because they are stronger, leading the user to try to get higher.

only under the care of a doctor. Many doctors recommend that medical marijuana patients initially use small dosages, and work one's way up to a dosage that works well for their illness or symptom—pain, for instance.

As with any drug that might make a person high, some people just want to get more and more high. This can result in addictive feelings or **withdrawal** symptoms. Some people believe that marijuana has become stronger over the years since the 1960s, when it was a popular drug among "hippies," or people in the counterculture. While some versions of cannabis today have higher concentrations of THC, most cannabis varieties are not that strong. Still, people can become **physically dependent** or **mentally dependent**, or even addicted, to marijuana and marijuana products, although the withdrawal symptoms are not considered as strong as withdrawal symptoms from drugs such as heroin, cocaine, opioids, alcohol, or even tobacco. Controlling marijuana use or not using marijuana at all is the best way to avoid becoming dependent or addicted. With that said, few people experience severe addiction to marijuana, and there is some debate over whether it's really addictive for most people.

Being safe as a teenager is the best way to go. Don't use marijuana until you're an adult to protect your brain. If you use medical marijuana with an adult guardian's permission and see a doctor regularly, you are in good hands because the dosage of the medicine is tightly controlled.

*Learn more about marijuana concentrates:*

## What to Do if You Think Someone May Be Addicted

Frequent marijuana use may not lead to severe withdrawal symptoms or cause a person to steal or lie just to get high. But marijuana use can cause anxiety in many people, or distract a person from goals in life when used often. Most people seeking to quit marijuana use have been daily users for about ten years, and have tried to quit using marijuana at least six times.

Cannabis use disorder (CUD) is a condition that was discovered in 2016, and that the National Institutes of Health (NIH) states is "common and often untreated." NIH notes

*Behavioral counseling is effective in helping teens quit using marijuana.*

that CUD can be part of other addictive disorders, as well as problems with behavior and disabilities. It also notes that long-term marijuana addiction is less severe than long-term heroin addiction or addiction to harder drugs. This does not mean that your friend or family member should not seek help if that person's life seems out of control. Cannabis use disorder (and other related disorders) may be worse for people who have been diagnosed with a psychiatric condition, and it may be combined with addiction to cocaine or alcohol, making it harder to treat.

If someone you know seems to be addicted to marijuana or marijuana concentrates, there are several ways to help. The first step is to talk to your friend or family member about his or her addiction and find out if that person is ready to quit or get help.

Behavioral therapies, such as drug counseling and therapy, are the most effective way to quit using marijuana and other drugs. Private and government-run drug-treatment facilities have been established to help those who think they are addicted to marijuana, other drugs, and alcohol. A person can simply call them to get in the program, which is often free if run by the state. Quitting marijuana may be easiest by avoiding situations where friends or relatives use it, and not falling back into old patterns. Support from family and friends is essential, but rehabilitation centers (with thirty- to ninety-day residential programs) can help in many ways, as can support groups for quitting, such as Marijuana Anonymous (https://www.marijuana-anonymous.org).

If you or someone you love is addicted to marijuana, a good place to start is by researching support groups on the internet, avoiding situations where marijuana may be used recreationally, and talking to your doctor or counselor. Needing marijuana to feel okay or function in the world means you may be addicted, unless you are using marijuana for medical reasons.

## Peer Pressure and the Gateway Drug Debate

Many teens use drugs under pressure from friends, or in a social setting, because they are trying to fit in with others. This is known as peer pressure, and although most teens are aware of it, it does still exist. Staying true to yourself and your own beliefs is the best way to avoid being influenced by peer pressure. Steering clear of other teens who do things you don't want to do is also a good strategy. As you come to know yourself better and gain confidence, peer pressure will become less of a problem, but that doesn't mean it isn't there.

*It's important to have quality friends who will never make you feel guilty because you do not want to use marijuana.*

Marijuana has been labeled a "**gateway drug**" by many anti-marijuana, or anti-drug, campaigns. The phrase "gateway drug" means that using marijuana leads to using other, harder drugs like methamphetamine, cocaine, ecstasy, or heroin. The National Institute on Drug Abuse (NIDA) found that sometimes marijuana use does come before the use of other hard drugs, and addiction to those harder drugs. There are also studies that say early use of marijuana in teens may lead to addiction to other drugs or alcohol later in life. Despite these findings, however, NIDA notes that "the majority of people who use marijuana do not go on to use other, 'harder' substances." So, it depends on the person, and using marijuana as a teen, although it may negatively affect your brain and learning processes, does not necessarily mean that a person will become addicted to heroin as an adult.

*Most people who use marijuana do not go on to use more dangerous drugs such as cocaine, but it does happen in some instances.*

## text-dependent questions

1. Is marijuana addictive?
2. Name three marijuana withdrawal symptoms.
3. Name three strong forms of marijuana concentrates.

## research project

In a group, collect members' experiences with marijuana that they are willing to talk about. Compare them to what you've learned in this chapter and talk about it with the group.

*It is now common to see marijuana dispensaries in many U.S. states.*

## words to understand

**adult-use:** Legal use of marijuana by people age twenty-one or older.

**brain development:** The way your brain grows and learns.

**clinical trials:** Controlled tests that study the effects of medicines on people or animals.

**epilepsy:** A condition of the brain that causes people to have seizures.

**maturity:** Gaining knowledge, being able to resist temptations, and see the "big picture" in life as you grow older.

# chapter 4

# Choosing to Use—or Not Use—Marijuana

## Living in a World Where Marijuana Is Increasingly Legal

If you live in a state or country where recreational or medical marijuana is legal, you may have seen billboards advertising it, stores that sell it, people smoking it in vape pens or joints on the street, or ads in newspapers or magazines in your hometown telling people where to go to buy it, or even offering coupons. If you don't live in a legal state or country, chances are marijuana legalization hasn't changed much for you and your community. Medical cannabis use is now legal in more than half of U.S. states. Some of these state governments may still be working on their cannabis programs, trying to make them safe for all members of the community and still help patients who experience relief by using medical cannabis. In most states, the minimum legal age for adult use of marijuana is twenty-one. In some states the age is as low as eighteen. Many doctors recommend that people do not use marijuana before the

*Marijuana laws vary by U.S. state. One thing is true in all states: it is illegal for anyone under age twenty-one to use recreational marijuana.*

age of twenty-five, because it may affect their learning processes later in life, and it may cause addiction. (Addiction is a brain disease in which a person has an overwhelming desire to use drugs, alcohol, or other substances, or engage in harmful acts or behaviors.) The truth is, we just don't know what the full effects of marijuana use during teen years are on **brain development**. We also don't know what the effects of adult use are. But we do know that as people become more mature, they make better life decisions, and they are better able to handle difficult situations that may lead to bad decisions.

*A growing number of parents are choosing to use medical marijuana to treat their children who are sick with diseases, disorders, or symptoms that traditional medicines can't seem to cure or improve.*

# How Many Adults Use Marijuana?

In the United States, more than half of adults over the age of eighteen have tried marijuana at least once, according to a Marist poll that was conducted in partnership with Yahoo. Almost half of those people continued to use marijuana after the first use. Many people who use marijuana are parents, and it is also popular among older adults, particularly those who lived through the 1960s when marijuana use was more acceptable than at other times in recent history. According to a Gallup poll, the majority of adults in the United States say they support using marijuana for medical treatments, but only half support recreational marijuana use. The country still has a long way to go to legalize recreational cannabis through the federal government, which has not made any use of marijuana legal. This means that the federal government can arrest anyone for marijuana possession or use, even though it usually does not do so because some states allow it.

As we discussed earlier, there are two aspects to marijuana use, medical use and **adult-use** (known as recreational use). Medical marijuana use involves using marijuana, concentrates, or extracts to treat pain or symptoms from chemotherapy treatment, Crohn's disease, or post-traumatic stress syndrome, to name a few. In most states, many doctors, nurses, and other medical professionals support the use of medical marijuana in proper dosages and under the supervision of a doctor. Recreational, or adult use, is an adult choice, however, and there are no doctors to show you how much to take or make sure you don't consume too much. When you use marijuana recreationally, you are taking a risk, just like you do when you drink alcohol or use other drugs. Marijuana affects people differently, and having the **maturity** to make good decisions about using marijuana or not is an important part of your life. Ultimately, whether or not your friends or family use it, the choice is up to you. This chapter can help you decide to make the choice that works for you when you are an adult.

# Medical Marijuana Treatments: How Do They Work?

Medical marijuana treatments for children or adults often start with a doctor consultation. In many states, doctors will discuss the options for medical marijuana treatments with interested parties, but some doctors may not. This is their choice, just as using marijuana as an adult or a parent will be yours. Just like any other medical treatment, some doctors support medical marijuana use, and some do not. Some are willing to talk about it whether they support it or not. If your doctor will not discuss this option, other doctors will. Information about medical marijuana on the internet is not always trustworthy. This is why consulting a doctor is so important. As adults, doctors can tell us how to use medical marijuana. Doctors are informed and well-educated. They know where to find the resources you need if you choose to use medical marijuana in the future.

MARIJUANA'S EFFECTS ON KIDS

MEDICAL MARIJUANA

WNCT 9 ON YOUR S

HEALTH WATCH

WNCT.com EFFECTS OF MEDICINAL MARIJUANA IN KIDS

*Learn more about the mental and physical effects of marijuana on teens:*

*It's important for teens to learn as much as they can about the benefits and harmful effects of marijuana so that they can make an educated choice about its use when they are adults.*

## Parents Who Treat Children with Medical Cannabis

Some parents choose to use marijuana to treat their children who have **epilepsy** and other diseases and disorders. Some people believe that this is wrong. But more and more cases such as that of Charlotte Figi (whose serious seizures were lessened by the use of CBD oil) are being shared on social media, by trusted news organizations, or through family and friends. For Charlotte (whom we learned about in *Marijuana in Society*), medical marijuana gave her a normal life. Are her parents wrong for trying this new type of marijuana treatment when nothing else worked? This is the type of hard call that many parents face. Many people who are sick with other diseases, disorders, or symptoms that traditional medicines have been unable to help with must also make hard choices. Medical marijuana has been used for centuries to relieve pain, and many people say it works better for them than medicines like opioids or even store-bought pain relievers. Parents must make their own decisions about medical treatment with marijuana, and decide whether it is a good option. And if you have a medical condition that does not seem to be getting better with the help of traditional medicine, using medical marijuana might be presented as an option if you live in a place where the use of medical marijuana is legal. In this instance, in collaboration with your parents, you will need to make an educated decision.

*It's a good idea to talk to your doctor if you have questions about marijuana.*

# U.S. States Where Recreational Marijuana Is Legal

Far fewer states have legalized the use of recreational marijuana. In a state where it is legal to use recreational marijuana, people don't have to go to doctors to get prescriptions or "medicine" in the form of marijuana or marijuana extracts. They can simply buy the products if they are twenty-one or older, and use them as they want to at home. Many people call this "self-treatment." This approach is growing in popularity as people realize the addictive nature of some pharmaceuticals, which may not even relieve their symptoms or pain. In states where recreational marijuana is legal, people can still obtain prescriptions from their doctors, and can often purchase more medical-grade marijuana, which may be designed to best treat a certain disease or symptom, such as pain. Medical-grade marijuana is not stronger than other forms of marijuana. In states where recreational marijuana is legal, making the decision to try medical marijuana instead of opioids for pain is happening more and more often for adults aged twenty-one and older, assisted by a doctor or not.

Talking to a doctor about medical marijuana, discussing the issues with other teens and adults, and doing careful research online at trusted websites are good ways to find out if medical marijuana is an option. Until there are more **clinical trials** of medical marijuana, though, it is hard to know for sure if medical marijuana will work for a disease or disorder. Still, parents with children suffering from severe seizure disorders and other conditions continue to use medical cannabis to help their children. For some, medical marijuana works, for others it does not. Many parents are willing to take the risk and stop using traditional prescription drugs to see if their children get better after being given medical marijuana.

## State and Federal Government Laws

Just because marijuana is legal in some U.S. states, does not mean that you cannot be punished, even as an adult, for using marijuana. Every state has its own laws about medical and recreational marijuana use. If you choose to use marijuana as an adult legally, you must know about these laws. The federal government may legalize medical marijuana in the future, but it is unknown if it will ever legalize recreational marijuana. Many more medical and scientific trials and studies will have to be done to prove that marijuana is as safe as traditional medicines. In the meantime, state laws let adults know what types of marijuana can be used, under what circumstances, where it can be used, and how much marijuana can be consumed, bought, or found in a person's home, car, or in their pockets, backpacks, or purses. Knowing your state's (or country's) laws is the best way to stay informed and make good decisions about marijuana use once you become an adult.

Marijuana laws change often. Organizations such as the Marijuana Policy Project (https://www.mpp.org) are excellent resources for learning about the marijuana laws in the United States. State government websites are another great resource, where you can learn which diseases, disorders, and symptoms can be treated with medical marijuana in your state. As laws change and more and more states allow medical marijuana and recreational marijuana (if it is voted legal), these websites will become more detailed, and help adults make good medical and recreational marijuana choices. If you live in a different country, visit government websites to learn about marijuana laws.

## Making Your Choice

Since you are not yet an adult, you don't have to decide yet about whether or not to use medical or recreational marijuana. You are too young to use marijuana legally, unless you have permission from a doctor and a parent or guardian (at the very least) to use medical marijuana. Many doctors and nurses recommend that you do not use marijuana until you are twenty-five, because it may negatively affect the development of your brain. It can slow the learning process, or affect the brain in ways that we haven't yet discovered. Over the next twenty years, marijuana research will advance, informing us more and more about the way marijuana interacts with

*Marijuana can negatively affect the development of your brain, as well as cause harmful physical side effects, so you should never use recreational marijuana if you are under the age of twenty-one.*

our brains and bodies. There may be good news and bad news, and we are likely to learn about both as we study the effects of marijuana on the human body. This is a good thing, but using marijuana before you are ready to handle the consequences or a bad reaction to it is not a good idea. You have time—and what we learn about marijuana over the next few decades will help us make medical marijuana use safer, regulate marijuana products to make them safer and easier to purchase, and help us understand the effects of marijuana.

Ultimately, the choice to use marijuana is up to you when you are an adult, but knowing the scientific and medical facts about how marijuana may affect your body and mind are an important part of making that decision. Your decision may also be affected by the experiences of family and friends, or the effects of marijuana on a disease or disorder that you have as an adult. Remember that using marijuana is a personal choice, and there is no such thing as conducting too much research. You can learn about marijuana until you are twenty-five, and still not know everything about it. Be safe, resist peer pressure, and learn as much as you can before making your decision.

*Scientists have yet to discover all of the potential medical benefits of marijuana.*

## text-dependent questions

1. At what age does your brain stop developing?
2. Is marijuana legal everywhere for medical use?
3. At what age is marijuana legal in most U.S. states?

## research project

Use the internet to learn more about how marijuana is being used to treat epilepsy. Watch videos, gather information from the Epilepsy Foundation, and write a short report on different treatments, including marijuana, and their effectiveness.

*A scientist conducts tests on cannabis in a laboratory. More medical studies are needed to determine the potential benefits and harmful effects of the drug.*

## words to understand

**convulsion:** A sudden, violent, irregular movement of arms, legs, or other parts of the body caused by brain disorders such as epilepsy.

**insomnia:** The inability to sleep.

**Jehovah's Witnesses:** A religious group that follows some beliefs shared by most Christians, but which believes that Jesus is the Son of God, but not part of a Trinity (Father, Son, Holy Ghost). They do not celebrate Christmas, and do not believe that the soul lives forever.

**traumatic:** An event or experience that is emotionally disturbing or distressing.

**treatment:** A substance or technique that is used to reduce the effects or eliminate illnesses, disorders, or medical problems.

# chapter 5

# The Limits and Future of Marijuana Science

## Teens and Marijuana Studies: Historical Barriers and Current Studies

Since the use of marijuana is legal only for adults age twenty-one and older (or eighteen in some places) in the United States, and only in some states, there have been few studies on the effects of marijuana on young people. The federal government protects children, teens, and adults from being included in medical trials of drugs, including marijuana, that might harm them. For this reason, medical studies on the effects of marijuana have been limited to adults who can decide for themselves and risk trying a new drug. Your parents are still legally responsible for you until you turn eighteen, and they can help you make decisions such as participating in a medical marijuana trial if you have a condition, disease, or disorder that it could help with. With the changing marijuana laws in many states, your doctor can also help you and your parents decide if a medical trial or a medical marijuana prescription is a good **treatment** strategy.

Historically, marijuana was classified as a Schedule I drug. This means that the U.S. government considered it as dangerous as heroin, cocaine, and some prescription drugs. As a result, medical studies were not allowed, and marijuana was not allowed for most researchers trying to find out about its effects. Today, the situation at the federal level is much the same, but states have been allowed to make their own decisions about medical and recreational marijuana, letting people who live in those states vote and decide whether treatments and use should be allowed. However, this does not change the federal government's stance—it still considers all forms

**The U.S. Drug Enforcement Agency plans to let more American universities grow medical marijuana for research trials.**

of marijuana as illegal. Because most medical trials of drugs such as marijuana are funded by the federal government, marijuana studies do not happen often. Since the dangers to children and teens in testing marijuana, whether medical or not, are greater, most studies are done with adults.

*Learn more about the benefits and risks of marijuana from a summary of a 2017 report by The National Academies of Sciences, Engineering, and Medicine:*

# Medical Migrants and Cannabidiol

Cannabidiol, or CBD, is a non-psychoactive component of marijuana, meaning that it won't make you feel "high." CBD has been shown to reduce the number of seizures in children with severe seizure disorders. Because of this, many states have legalized CBD in some form. In states where medical marijuana is still illegal, getting treatment for children or teens can be very difficult. If marijuana is illegal, then finding CBD oil can be hard for these families, who often must order it from out of state and risk getting caught by law enforcement. Another alternative is to move to a state where medical marijuana is legal. These families are called "medical migrants," and many have moved to states such as Colorado, Washington, and Oregon, where marijuana is legal and CBD oil is widely available. *The New York Times* reported that one-hundred families moved to Colorado in 2014 to access seizure-controlling medicines such as CBD oil. *Fortune* reported that people have been moving to Oregon from all over the world, including a family from Ireland whose two-year-old son had twenty seizures a day until he tried CBD oil. Now he doesn't have any.

## Future Studies on Teens and Marijuana

Until the U.S. federal government removes marijuana from the Drug Enforcement Administration's (DEA) Controlled Substances Act, or changes marijuana from a Schedule I drug to a Schedule II, III, IV, or V drug, marijuana remains illegal and considered a highly-addictive drug along with heroin, cocaine, and methamphetamine. Many pro-cannabis organizations (such as the Marijuana Policy Project, Americans for Safe Access, and Marijuana Majority), politicians, and medical professionals have been trying for years to remove marijuana from Schedule I of the DEA's

# Marijuana Research Around the World

While debate continues in the United States over whether medical marijuana should be legal, other countries have moved past this decision and legalized medical marijuana, allowing research and medicine for their citizens and others all over the world. Medical marijuana has been legal in Canada since 2001, but very few companies can grow the plant for patients. Patients get medicine mailed to them, and there are no legal dispensaries in Canada (this may change in the near future). Researchers in Canada are trying to find out how marijuana affects memory, attention, and thinking; the ability to drive; pregnancy; and breathing. Canadian researchers found that marijuana is addictive, that it can make it harder to function in school, and that it may cause psychosis or other disorders in teens.

Dr. Raphael Mechoulam, one of the Israeli scientists who discovered CBD and THC, lives and works in Israel today, where medical marijuana research is legal and supported by the government and its Ministry of Health. Israeli researchers are studying how medical marijuana can help autistic children and adults, as well as how marijuana can be used to treat other illnesses and conditions.

Scientists in Australia are also researching medical marijuana, and countries such as Germany pay for research in Israel because it costs less than conducting research in their own countries.

list of drugs. This would allow patients and people to use it for treatments instead of worrying that they will get arrested. In August 2016, the DEA announced that it would keep marijuana listed as a highly-addictive and dangerous drug, but it would allow more people to research marijuana's effects. The DEA plans to do this by letting more universities in the United States grow medical marijuana for research trials. It also decided to allow legal growing of industrial hemp in states that vote for it. Hemp has very low amounts of THC and cannot be used to get "high." It can be used to make rope, textiles, paper, and other products.

## Breakthroughs in Marijuana Science

Many people want medical marijuana to be legalized in order to help people with illnesses and disorders that can't be treated with other drugs, or those who are still

*Marijuana research is conducted in the United States, Canada, Israel, Australia, and other countries.*

in pain despite taking traditional medications. The side effects of opioids and other medicines prescribed by doctors make life unpleasant for many people. Medical marijuana is a natural alternative that does not cause as many side effects, and can help people feel better very quickly and inexpensively. Beginning with Dr. Raphael Mechoulam's breakthrough discovery of CBD and THC in the 1960s, science began taking medical marijuana seriously. As medical marijuana became legal in more and more states, people from all walks of life began to try it and found that it worked well for some health diseases and disorders. Medical marijuana helps people with pain from accidents, diseases, and arthritis, providing relief when other medicines do not. Here are a few examples of the benefits of medical marijuana:

## Post-Traumatic Stress Disorder and Marijuana

Post-traumatic stress disorder (PTSD) is a disorder that affects many people who have gone through a **traumatic** or life-threatening event, including military combat, a natural disaster like a hurricane, a bad car accident, sexual assault, attempted murder, or rape. People with PTSD have not recovered well from these events, and may feel on edge all the time, or nervous even months or years after the event. Many people with PTSD have **insomnia**, and may have difficulty with work, school, or relationships with family and friends. They may be depressed or on edge, feel hopeless, feel angry, have drug or alcohol problems, have trouble finding or keeping jobs, and have difficulty in relationships.

Many people with PTSD find that using medical marijuana helps with their symptoms, and allows them to relax and avoid repetitive thoughts about the traumatic event. Medical marijuana can also improve the sleep of people with PTSD.

More than 40,000 U.S. military veterans have been diagnosed with PTSD and cannabis use disorder. In Canada, up to 10 percent of war-zone veterans have PTSD. Since marijuana cannot be legally tested on most people, we don't know for sure whether it can help people with PTSD. Some veterans believe it helps their symptoms, and many U.S. states, as well as Canada and other countries, have passed medical marijuana laws that allow people to take medical marijuana for PTSD. For veterans in states where medical marijuana is legal for PTSD treatment, the choice is up to them.

*Marijuana is used to treat the symptoms of post-traumatic stress disorder (PTSD). Above, a psychologist talks with a soldier who has been diagnosed with PTSD after serving in a war zone.*

## Israel's Holocaust Survivors and Marijuana

The Holocaust was an event that took place from 1933 to 1945 during World War II. When the Nazi party took over Germany in 1933, it believed that Jewish people were not as good as Germans, and that they should be killed. The Nazis also believed the same thing about the Romani people from Romania, people with disabilities, Polish people, Russians, **Jehovah's Witnesses**, and homosexuals. During the Holocaust, the Nazis forced people to take trains or walk to concentration camps, where they were forced to live in horrible conditions and systematically killed in a variety of ways. More than six million Jewish people were killed during the Holocaust, and almost 700,000 Jewish people emigrated to Israel after the Allies ended war in the European Theatre on May 9, 1945.

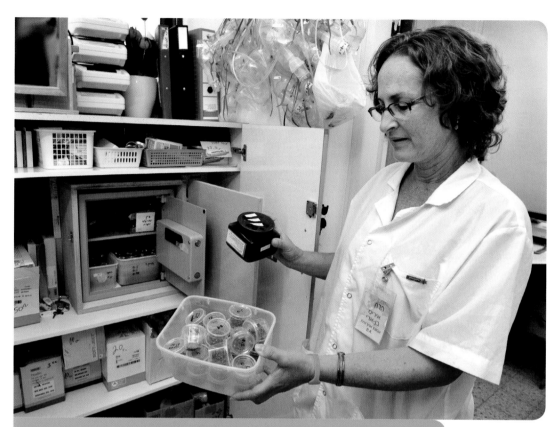

*In Israel, medical marijuana is given to the elderly—some whom survived the Holocaust—to help them feel less anxiety, sleep better, and increase their appetites.*

The terror experienced by people who survived the Holocaust is extreme. A medical marijuana company in Israel called Tikun Olam has started Project 70 Plus for elderly patients, including those who live in nursing homes. Many of these patients are Holocaust survivors and suffer from PTSD, insomnia, and appetite issues. Marijuana can help people feel less anxiety, sleep better, and increase appetite. Tikun Olam conducted an observational study of nineteen nursing home residents. It gave medical marijuana in a vaporizer, or as powder or oil. The nursing home residents ate more and gained weight, slept longer and better, and were able to stop some use of other medicines such as painkillers and antidepressants. In an interview about the study in *Hadassah Magazine*, Inbal Sikorin, the nursing home's head nurse said, "We've already learned to prolong life, marijuana adds to the quality of life."

# Marijuana and Pain Relief

Marijuana has been used for pain relief for thousands of years. Many doctors believe that it should be prescribed instead of highly-addictive opioids that may not help with pain as much as marijuana. One-hundred million people in the United States live with chronic pain, according to the National Institutes of Health, and opioids do not help that much. People who take opioids before and after surgery for pain may become addicted to them, even though they may not provide relief from pain. More than 14,000 Americans died from overdosing on prescribed painkillers in 2014, according to the Centers for Disease Control and Prevention. Until the U.S. federal government reschedules marijuana, most doctors cannot prescribe medical marijuana for chronic pain.

## Childhood Epilepsy and CBD

Epilepsy is a condition of the brain that causes people to have seizures. A seizure is a **convulsion** of the body that is caused by a surge of electrical activity in the brain and usually lasts for a short time. For people, and especially children with severe seizure disorders, seizures may be strong, last a long time, and happen very often. Because a seizure stops people from doing anything, and causes their bodies to convulse or spasm, seizures can keep them from getting dressed, doing homework, talking, playing, eating, drinking, and sleeping. Not all seizures can be noticed, but if a child or person has a severe seizure disorder, it can make that person's life, and the lives of their family members and friends, very hard. More than sixty-five million people in the world have epilepsy, according to Citizens United for Research in Epilepsy. One-third of these people live with uncontrollable seizures because no traditional treatments work for them.

A major breakthrough in medical marijuana science has helped reduce seizures in many children with severe epilepsy. The Epilepsy Foundation says that cannabis can be helpful in seizure control, especially for Lennox-Gastaut Syndrome and Dravet Syndrome in children. Because CBD oil does not make people high, it is a good choice for treatment of children, and it is the most-approved medical marijuana treatment for disorders across the United States. Dr. Orrin Devinsky, director of New York University's Langone Comprehensive Epilepsy Center, says that cannabis was used in 1800 B.C. in Sumeria (now southern Iraq) to treat epilepsy, and that nineteenth century neurologists used Indian hemp to treat it, too. Pharmaceutical medications usually don't work for people with Dravet Syndrome, and one-fifth of patients die before they are twenty years old. Most children with Dravet Syndrome who receive medical marijuana experience about 40 percent fewer seizures, and some have no more seizures at all. Almost all children have side effects, like being sleepy, less hungry, having diarrhea, and vomiting. Many, but not all, families believe the side effects are not so bad that they would stop using CBD oil to treat their child's seizures.

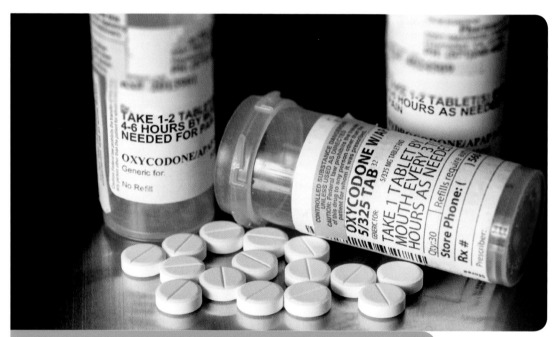

*Marijuana is increasingly used as a pain-relief alternative to highly-addictive opioids such as Oxycodone.*

## A Promising Future

Medical marijuana science and research is really just in its early stages in the United States. Although it should only be conducted by professional researchers and scientists, those who live in places where marijuana is legal are also experimenting with the use of marijuana to treat various health conditions. But they should do so very carefully—and only if they are adults. Medical marijuana should still be used while in a doctor's care, and in a safe way, but the plant and its extracts hold great promise for the future of medicine throughout the world.

## text-dependent questions

1. Which Israeli doctor and scientist discovered CBD and THC?
2. Why is it hard to research marijuana's effects in the United States?
3. What disorders or symptoms do people take medical marijuana for?

## research project

Study the medical marijuana laws in your state or country. What conditions allow medical marijuana treatment? (Hint: look at state government websites.)

**adult-use cannabis:** The recreational use of cannabis by those over the age of twenty-one.

**cannabidiol (CBD):** A chemical compound found in the cannabis plant that is non-psychoactive. It is known for its medical and pain relief properties.

**cannabinoid:** Any of various chemical compounds (such as THC) from the cannabis or marijuana plant that produces a euphoric feeling, or "high."

**cannabis clubs:** Marijuana growing and consumption cooperatives (a group that is owned and run by its members) that exist in countries such as Uruguay and Spain to provide cannabis users with marijuana products and a place to use those products.

**cannabis strains:** Varieties of cannabis plants that are developed to have different properties and potencies.

**clinical trials:** Experiments with unproven medications that may or may not help a patient get better.

**dabbing:** A somewhat controversial method of cannabis flash-vaporization. It has very strong effects on the user.

**decriminalization:** The legal term for getting rid of or reducing criminal charges for having or using cannabis.

**delta-9-tetrahydrocannabinol (THC):** A natural chemical compound found in the flowers of the marijuana plant. It produces a feeling of euphoria and a psychoactive reaction, or "high," when marijuana is eaten or smoked.

**dopamine:** A naturally occurring chemical in the human body that increases pleasurable feelings in the mind and body.

**drug trafficking:** A global illegal trade involving the growth, manufacture, distribution, and sale of substances, such as cannabis, that are subject to drug prohibition laws.

**edible:** A food made or infused (cooked or otherwise prepared) with cannabis extracts (portions of the plant, including seeds or flowers).

**endocannabinoid system:** A group of cannabinoid receptors found in the brain and central and peripheral nervous systems of mammals that help control appetite, pain, mood, and memory.

**euphoria:** A feeling of intense well-being and happiness.

**extracts:** Portions of the marijuana plant, including seeds or flowers.

**hash:** A solid or resinous extract of cannabis.

**hemp:** A cannabis plant grown for its fiber and used to make rope, textiles, paper, and other products.

**ingest:** To take food, drink, or another substance into the body.

**lethargy:** Lack of enthusiasm and energy; a common side effect of cannabis use.

**Marihuana Tax Act of 1937:** A marijuana taxation act that led to the prohibition of cannabis in the United States during much of the twentieth century.

**marijuana:** A cannabis plant that is smoked or consumed as a psychoactive (mind-altering) drug.

**marijuana dispensary:** A place where people can buy recreational or medical cannabis. Dispensaries are tightly controlled by the government.

**marijuana oil:** Liquid that is extracted from the hemp plant and placed in either capsule form or combined with foods or drinks. CBD is most commonly consumed as an oil.

**medical cannabis identification card:** A document issued by a state where it is legal to use medical cannabis; the card indicates that a patient may use, buy, or have medical cannabis at home, on his or her person, or both.

**neuroprotectant:** A substance that repairs and protects the nervous system, its cells, structure, and function.

**neurotransmitter:** Chemicals that communicate information in the human body.

**opiates:** Substances derived from the opium poppy plant such as heroin.

**opium:** A highly addictive narcotic drug that is created by collecting and drying the milky juice that comes from the seed pods of the poppy plant.

**prohibition:** The action of forbidding something, especially by law.

**propaganda:** False information that is created to influence people.

**prosecution:** The conducting of legal proceedings against someone if it is believed that they broke the law.

**psychoactive drug:** A drug that affects the mind.

**psychosis:** Detachment from reality.

**receptors:** Groups of specialized cells that can convert energy into electrical impulses.

**repeal:** To get rid of a law or congressional act.

**shatter:** Cannabis concentrate that looks like colored glass.

**social cannabis use:** The use of cannabis in social settings, whether in public or private.

**tar:** A toxic byproduct of cigarette or marijuana smoking.

**tincture:** A medicine made by dissolving a drug in alcohol, vinegar, or glycerites.

**topicals:** Cannabis-infused lotions, balms, and salves that relieve pain and aches at the application site on the body.

**vaporizer:** A device that is used to turn water or medicated liquid into a vapor for inhalation.

**War on Drugs:** An anti-drug campaign started in the United States in 1971 by then-president Richard Nixon. Its goal was to fight drug abuse and shipments of illegal drugs to the U.S. from Latin America, Mexico, and other places.

# Index

# Photo Credits

# Further Reading & Internet Resources

Backes, Michael. *Cannabis Pharmacy: The Practical Guide to Medical Marijuana*. Revised ed. New York: Black Dog & Leventhal, 2017.

Compton, Michael T. *Marijuana and Mental Health*. Washington, D.C.: American Psychiatric Association Publishing, 2016.

Hudak, John. *Marijuana: A Short History*. Washington, D.C.: Brookings Institution Press, 2016.

Lee, Martin A. *Smoke Signals: A Social History of Marijuana: Medical, Recreational and Scientific*. New York: Scribner, 2013.

National Academies of Sciences, Engineering, and Medicine and Health and Medicine Division. *The Health Effects of Cannabis and Cannabinoids: The Current State of Evidence and Recommendations for Research*. Washington, D.C.: National Academies Press, 2017.

## Internet Resources

**http://www.ncsl.org/research/health/state-medical-marijuana-laws.aspx** This is the official website of the National Conference for State Legislatures. It provides information on current U.S. medical cannabis laws.

**https://www.drugabuse.gov/drugs-abuse/marijuana** This is the official U.S. government website for marijuana created by the National Institute on Drug Abuse (NIDA). It includes a description of marijuana and its health effects, as well as statistics and information on trends and research.

**https://www.drugabuse.gov/publications/marijuana-facts-teens/want-to-know-more-some-faqs-about-marijuana** This website from the NIDA answers frequently asked questions about marijuana such as: How does marijuana work? Does marijuana use lead to other drugs? What happens if you smoke marijuana? What does marijuana do to the brain?

**https://www.cdc.gov/marijuana/factsheets/teens.htm** This website from the Centers for Disease Control and Prevention provides information on marijuana's effects on teens.

**https://www.webmd.com/brain/ss/slideshow-medical-marijuana** This website provides answers to frequently asked questions such as: What is medical marijuana? How does marijuana work on the brain? What are the short- and long-term side effects?

## About the Author:

Julie Nelson is a cannabis industry consultant and freelance writer and editor, and a native Coloradan. She holds a B.A. in creative writing from the University of Colorado at Boulder, a master's in technical communication from Minnesota State University at Mankato, and is pursuing a degree in medical communication from Boston University. Julie has written and researched extensively in the areas of medical, technical, academic, and political writing. Her experience in the medical and recreational cannabis industry in Colorado is what drew her to this project, and the chance to spread accurate, researched, and correct information about the cannabis plant in a way that students and instructors might understand. Julie also writes short fiction, children's books, and short horror fiction, and her work has been published in numerous anthologies and online. Julie's journalism and other writing on the cannabis industry has been published in *Bust*, and online at 3C Cannabis Consulting, Mass Roots, Green Lotus Hemp, and many other websites. Julie lives in Denver, Colorado, with her family and enjoys every season to the fullest.

## Video Credits

**Chapter 1:** Learn more about the negative effects of marijuana on the teenage brain, and the debate about legalization: http://x-qr.net/1EWw

**Chapter 2:** Watch the effects of marijuana on drivers: http://x-qr.net/1GJc

**Chapter 3:** Learn more about marijuana concentrates: http://x-qr.net/1Dfm

**Chapter 4:** Learn more about the mental and physical effects of marijuana on teens: http://x-qr.net/1Dz1

**Chapter 5:** Learn more about the benefits and risks of marijuana from a summary of a 2017 report by The National Academies of Sciences, Engineering, and Medicine: http://x-qr.net/1HEA